101
things to see
in Devon

Robert Hesketh

GW00648551

Bossiney Books

First published 2020 by
Bossiney Books Ltd, 67 West Busk Lane, Otley, LS21 3LY
www.bossineybooks.com

ISBN 978-1-906474-81-2

Acknowledgements
The maps are by Graham Hallowell
All photographs are by the author, www.roberthesketh.co.uk
except those for places 6 & 56 which are from the publishers' collection

Printed in Great Britain by Deltor, Saltash PL12 6LZ

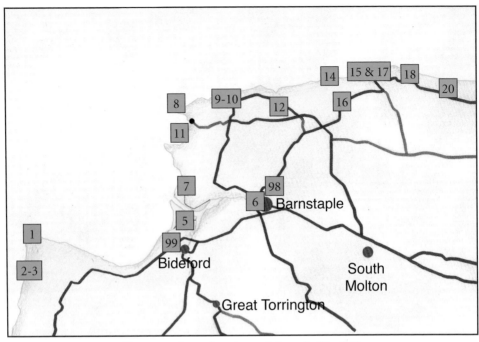

The approximate locations of places in North Devon

What's included?

We decided to exclude anywhere with an admission charge, which meant omitting some fantastic places, from Clovelly in the north to Kent's Cavern in the south. We have included some places where there's something worth seeing from the outside without paying, such as castles, cliff railways and even a couple of pubs.

Some museums request a donation, but the amount is at your discretion. We hope the selection will help you enjoy your holiday to the full without great expense.

The information given was accurate at the time of going to press, but parking and entry charges are subject to change.

North

1 Hartland Point

Hartland Point's wild seascape is a short walk from its car park and seasonal café. The views into Cornwall, along Bideford Bay and north to Lundy are breathtaking. Despite having had a lighthouse since 1874, the jagged rocks 100 m (330 ft) below remain a serious hazard to shipping. Hartland Point is a migration point for birds in spring and autumn. Look out too for seals.

2 Speke's Mill Mouth

A 1.25 km (1 mile) walk south along the Coast Path from Hartland Quay leads to Devon's largest waterfall. In return for a fairly modest effort, this walk includes some of Devon's most spectacular coastal scenery. The vista along the cliffs and far into Cornwall is stunning.

3 Hartland Quay

Hartland Quay is backed by North Devon's most dramatic rock formations. It has a hotel/pub offering refreshments, a shop and an excellent museum, which explains the area's rich ecology and dramatic geology and gives a vivid impression of the dangers of sailing and trading on this rugged coast. Hartland Quay handled a variety of cargoes and thrived from Queen Elizabeth I's time until damaged by storms in the late nineteenth century.

4 Seals

Morte and Hartland Points are among the best places in Devon to see seals. Atlantic or grey seals have a British population of around 120,000. Mature males grow to over 2 metres and weigh well over 200kg.

5 Appledore

Appledore's charming narrow streets mainly date from its 17-18th century heyday as a port for the North America trade. The Quay overlooks the beautiful Taw/Torridge estuary. Appledore is home to several artists, drawn by the lovely local seascapes and North Devon's clarity of light.

6 Butcher's Row and the Pannier Market, Barnstaple

Butcher's Row stands opposite to the Pannier Market. Both were built in 1855 using Bath stone (now painted) for the Butcher's Row arcades, mirroring the Pannier Market's brick arcades. Originally it contained 33 butchers' shops, but now houses various small businesses from cafés to bakeries, confectionery, cheese, beer and hardware shops.

7 Saunton Sands and Braunton Burrows

Behind the great expanse of Saunton Sands, a superb surfing beach, lies Braunton Burrows, one of Britain's largest and most impressive sand dune systems. From spring to early autumn it has a continuous succession of flowering plants, over 600 species.

4

8 Morte Point

This is a pleasant 1.5km (1 mile) walk from Mortehoe; it provides magnificent views across Morte Bay with Bideford Bay beyond. The views east to Rockham Beach and Bull Point Lighthouse are equally impressive. Mortehoe's Heritage Centre offers a cameo of local history: displays of farming, tourism and, above all, shipwrecks. Morte Point's sharp rocks have claimed many ships, including five in the winter of 1852 alone.

9 Ilfracombe's Victorian architecture

A superb setting amidst the cliffs helped the long established port of Ilfracombe develop into North Devon's leading Victorian resort. Centred on its beautiful harbour, where fishing boats mingle with yachts and smaller pleasure craft, Ilfracombe remains predominantly Victorian in buildings and ambience, though enriched by its earlier history, including the medieval chapel of St Nicholas on Lantern Hill.

10 Verity sculpture

The controversial statue 'Verity' was created by Damien Hirst. She stands at the entrance to Ilfracombe Harbour, an impressive 20.25 m (66.4 ft) tall. Hirst described Verity as a 'modern allegory of truth and justice'. She holds a sword aloft, while carrying the scale of justice and standing on a pile of law books. She is pregnant and half her internal anatomy, including the foetus, is exposed.

5

11 Woolacombe

North Devon's huge sandy beaches are popular with families and surfers alike. Woolacombe, along with Saunton, Croyde, Putsborough, Coombesgate and Westward Ho!, are its leading surf beaches. Equipment can be bought or hired from local surf shops .

12 Pack of Cards, Combe Martin

This unique inn was built by George Ley in 1690. After winning handsomely at cards he promised 'an everlasting monument to Lady Luck'. The Pack is inspired by a deck of 52 playing cards: 52 feet square, it has four storeys — the four suits. There are 52 windows and 52 steps in the staircase; 13 doors on each floor and 13 fireplaces. The four chimneys on the top floor represent the four kings, the four below the four queens. Visit the Pack's museum for more details.

13 Exmoor Coast Path

Devon's Exmoor coast meets the sea in a series of high cliffs, including Great Hangman near Combe Martin, the highest point on the South West Coast Path. Good vantage points to park and walk include Holdstone Down, Woody Bay and Countisbury (Barna Barrow).

14 Heddon's Mouth Cleave

A beautiful level path, 1.7km (1 mile) long, links the National Trust car park and Heddon's Mouth. Heddon's Mouth Cleave is a steep sided valley cut by a fast flowing river and lined by towering cliffs.

15 Valley of Rocks

The Valley of Rocks provides an exceptional if not unique example of full glacial action in Devon. Spectacular tors and other frost-riven features mark the valley's sides, which have been further dismembered by coastal cliff recession. The Valley of Rocks may be explored on foot from its car park, or reached by the beautiful, near level North Walk (2 km/ 1³/4 miles) from Lynton. North Walk provides marvellous views of Exmoor's high cliffs and over to South Wales.

16 Lynton & Barnstaple Railway

Woody Bay station was part of the Lynton and Barnstaple Railway (1898-1935). Now restored in Southern Railway style, complete with delightful period paraphernalia of art deco posters, red fire buckets and leather luggage, Woody Bay offers visitors steam-hauled rides in restored vintage carriages. The station provides light refreshments and railway souvenirs.

17 Lynton Cliff Railway

Lynton's unique cliff railway was built in 1890. It simply works by gravity, balancing the weight of its two cars on a continuous pulley system. With its tank filled with 3200 litres (700 gallons) of water from the West Lyn, the top car descends, pulling the lighter car 261 m up the inclined plane from Lynmouth, on a 58% gradient. Reaching the bottom of the slope, the first car dumps its load and the process is reversed.

18 Watersmeet

Watersmeet, with its deep wooded gorges and waterfalls, is always impressive, especially after rain and in autumn colours. The 3 km (2 mile) riverside path from Lynmouth to the National Trust's Watersmeet tea room and information centre is one of Exmoor's finest walks. Alternatively, drive up the A39 towards Barbrook and use the Watersmeet car park.

19 Exmoor Ponies

Short and stocky with thick coats, Exmoor ponies are typically dark bay or brown, reminiscent of the earthy colours in ancient cave paintings. Mealy markings on the muzzle are characteristic. Eleven privately owned pony herds roam as semi-feral livestock over the Exmoor commons, contributing to natural pasture habitats. Foals are born in spring. In autumn, the ponies are rounded up, inspected and marked, then returned to the moor for winter.

20 Lorna Doone Farm and Badgworthy

R D Blackmore set his swashbuckling novel *Lorna Doone* on Exmoor. The attractive and gentle walk along Badgworthy Water from Lorna Doone Farm (shop and inn) is at the heart of the story. It is 1.25 km (3/4 mile) along the riverside path to refreshments at Cloud Farm and a further 2.4 km (1 1/2 miles) to the place Blackmore imagined as the lair of the dastardly Doones. In reality, it is a deserted medieval village.

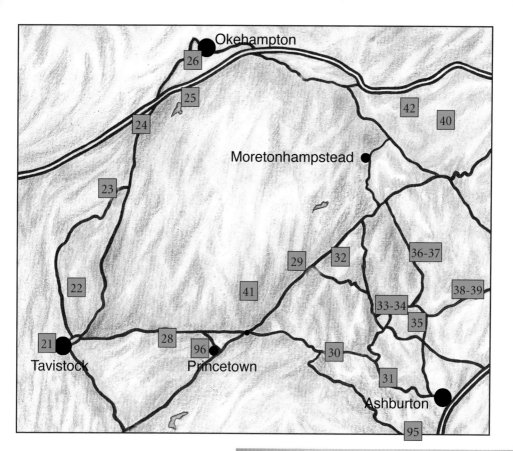

Dartmoor and around

21 Tavistock: Drake Statue

JE Boehm's 1883 bronze statue of Sir Francis Drake stands at the far end of Plymouth Road. With his sword, poignard and globe, symbols of his life as admiral and navigator, Sir Francis (1542-96) strikes a commanding pose. Beneath are scenes from his life: Queen Elizabeth knighting him on board ship, Drake playing bowls on Plymouth Hoe and his burial at sea. A replica Drake statue stands on Plymouth Hoe.

22 Brent Tor

Brent Tor is a landmark for miles around. Crowned with a tiny Norman church and the remains of an Iron Age hill fort, it is composed of volcanic breccia and pillow lava. It has wonderful views onto a range of Dartmoor tors and over the patchwork fields of the Tamar Valley to the heights of Bodmin Moor. Access is by footpath from the car park.

23 Lydford Castle

Lydford Castle was built in 1195 to incarcerate royal prisoners. It was later a Stannary Gaol, imprisoning people for tin-mining offences and 'Lydford Law' became a by-word for injustice. It was described as 'one of the most heinous, contagious and detestable places in the realm' (1512). Open daily (English Heritage, free).

24 Highwayman pub at Sourton

A cross between a fairy tale and an antiques shop, the medieval Highwayman Inn is unique. Enter through the stagecoach lobby (the genuine article) to an Aladdin's Cave of swords and shields, a stag's head, horse brasses, blacksmith's bellows, church pews, sewing machines and Old Mother Hubbard's shoe.

25 Meldon Viaduct

Meldon Viaduct, a triumph of Victorian engineering, was built in 1874 to cross the West Okement. After the 1963 Beeching Report, the Bude line was closed and the Exeter-Plymouth line was cut back to Meldon Quarry. The viaduct is now part of the Granite Way, an 11km (7 mile) cycle/walkway that follows the railway towards Lydford and forms part of Cycle Route 27.

26 Okehampton Castle

This is Devon's largest castle, enjoying a strong position on a spur of rock overlooking the West Okement river and guarding the main road from Exeter into Cornwall. It was built shortly after the Norman Conquest and held by the Courtenays, Earls of Devon, until Henry Courtenay was executed in 1539. The ruins can be seen from the outside, or visited (English Heritage, entry fee).

27 Dartmoor ponies

Some 3000 ponies roam the moor all year round and help make Dartmoor the unique place it is. One of Britain's nine native breeds along with the Exmoor (page 8), the true Dartmoor is short (12.2 hands, 1.27m, or less) and stocky with a thick mane and tail and a dense winter coat. Special breeding programmes have improved the stock in recent years. It is illegal to feed them.

28 Merrivale

Merrivale's remarkable Bronze Age antiquities include two double stone rows over 200m long, each with a standing stone. There are seven cairns, the foundations of partially enclosed round house settlements and a stone circle. Whilst the stone rows date from around 2000 BC, the rest may be slightly later and the hut circles are tentatively dated to 1500 BC.

29 Postbridge

Postbridge is the most impressive of Dartmoor's many clapper bridges, with a span of 13 m (43 ft) and exceptionally tall stone piers. Postbridge stands beside a late 18th century turnpike trust arched bridge.

30 Dartmeet

The East and West Dart rivers converge just below the road bridge at Dartmeet, which has convenient parking and refreshments at Badger's Holt. Cross the road bridge and walk downstream to see the arc of stepping stones. Easily passable in dry months, they can be tricky or even impassable after rain.

31 New Bridge

New Bridge (parking and toilets) dates from the 15th century, a time when wealth from locally produced tin and wool encouraged bridge building. It was already old in 1645, when the Sessions ordered £13 for its repairs.

32 Grimspound

Grimspound is Dartmoor's most impressive prehistoric site, a high double walled enclosure of 1.6 ha protecting 24 hut circles. It was built as a pound to keep domestic animals in and predators out. With a little imagination, step back into the Bronze Age when Grimspound sheltered a community of perhaps fifty people, who herded sheep and cattle, grew crops and hunted game. Access is by a 400 m long path from a layby at SX 697809, 2.2 km/1 1/2 miles south of B3212.

33 Widecombe

As well as its tree-shaded green, two inns, cafés and quality gift shops, this beautiful granite village has a church of exceptional dignity. The 'cathedral of the moor' was enlarged in the 15th and 16th centuries with profits from tinning. The 16th century Church House serves as a National Trust shop and local information centre as well as village hall.

34 Widecombe Fair

The comic folk song spread Widecombe Fair's fame far beyond Dartmoor. It is one of Devon's largest festivals, held in September and celebrating traditional Dartmoor life. There are country crafts, folk music, stalls selling local produce, country games, sheep-dog displays, parades of hounds and vintage tractors, gun dog and dog agility competitions and much more besides, including the Dartmoor Hill Pony Display Team (photo right). Refreshments all day.

35 Buckland Beacon and the Ten Commandments Stones

From Buckland Beacon the views stretch over much of southern Dartmoor, the South Hams and on to the Channel. Northwards, Dartmoor's lofty tors ride the horizon. Below is the deep and thickly wooded valley of the Double Dart and Buckland's pretty church, dwarfed by the vast landscape. The Ten Commandments stones on Buckland Beacon were carved in 1928 by a local mason who camped here for several weeks.

13

36 Hound Tor

Hound Tor's dramatic rock piles are superb examples of vertically and horizontally weathered granite. According to a legend which helped inspire Sir Arthur Conan Doyle's *The Hound of the Baskervilles*, Hound Tor is a pack of hounds turned to stone when their master, Bowerman, was punished for hunting with them on the Sabbath.

37 Hound Tor medieval village

Hound Tor's medieval village (600m SE of the car park, at SX746788) is among 130 abandoned Dartmoor settlements. It was most probably established during the early medieval expansion of population and settlement and abandoned following the catastrophic population decline provoked by the Great Famine, 1315 and the Black Death, 1348-9.

38 Haytor Rocks

All Dartmoor tors have individual profiles and Haytor Rocks is the most recognisable. At 457m (1508ft), it is one of the moor's finest viewpoints, with a panorama including many Dartmoor tors.

39 Haytor Granite Tramway

Effectively Devon's first railway, the tramway used hand cut granite rails and horse-drawn wagons, carrying up to three tonnes of stone from the five quarries on Haytor Down to waiting barges on the canal at Teigngrace, 13.6km (8 1/2 miles) distant. Haytor granite was used in building London Bridge and the British Museum Library.

40 Teign Gorge and Castle Drogo

The spectacular Teign Gorge can be explored from two paths which make a circuit from Fingle Bridge, a 17th century granite packhorse bridge. The 'Hunter's Path' gives dramatic views onto Dartmoor and vertiginous perspectives of the gorge, whilst the bankside 'Fisherman's Path' follows the rushing Teign. Off the Hunter's Path is Castle Drogo (National Trust), England's newest castle. It was designed by Sir Edwin Lutyens and built in local granite between 1910 and 1930 as a luxury home for grocery tycoon Julius Drew.

41 Wistman's Wood

Wistman's Wood is one of three small remnants of the oak woods that covered most of Dartmoor before Neolithic and Bronze Age clearances. Gnarled and stunted oaks survive here because they grow among granite boulders, which defend them from grazing animals. Access by footpath from Two Bridges car park, SX609751, 2km (1 1/4 miles) each way.

42 Spinsters' Rock

Spinster's Rock is the best surviving example in Devon of a Neolithic burial chamber, erected around 3500 to 2500 BC. The stones collapsed in 1862 and were then re-erected. Legend has it that three spinsters built the monument one morning before breakfast. Location SX701907, signed on a minor road off A382 near Drewsteignton.

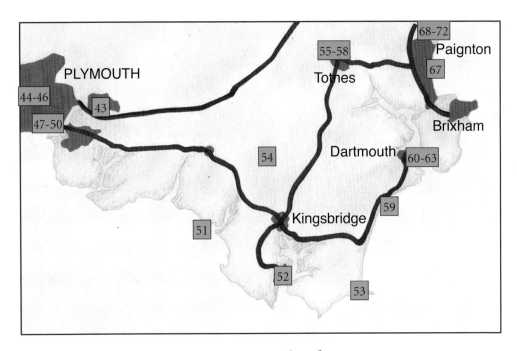

South

43 Plympton St Maurice

The historic heart of Plympton has 1100 years of recorded history and predates Plymouth. Its 12th century motte and bailey castle gives a good view of the old town. Plympton's Guildhall and historic Butterwalk stand in Fore Street. Sir Joshua Reynolds, the 18th century portrait painter, was educated at Plympton Grammar School.

44 Royal Albert Bridge

IK Brunel's 2200 ft long Royal Albert Bridge was completed in 1859 after six years intensive toil using bold and experimental technology, which included building the piers at pressure below water level. The bridge still carries mainline trains over the Tamar – a tribute to Brunel's skill and his wise choice of

16

corrosion-resistant wrought iron. It stands next to the Tamar Road Bridge, opened 102 years later.

45 Devonport Guildhall

This architectural gem (1822) by John Foulston is the centrepiece of Ker Street, well complemented by the neighbouring Greek Doric column and Foulston's Egyptian House. Grecian in inspiration, its four column Doric portico has classical beauty and proportion. Rather weirdly, it is surmounted by the figure of Britannia – who was completely unknown to the classical world as her invention lay far in the future.

46 Royal William Yard

The Yard (1835) was designed by Sir John Rennie in limestone and granite and named after William IV. It was used by the Royal Navy as a victualling yard until 1992. Now open to the public, it has restaurants, cafés, shops, a hotel, a gallery and a programme of events, including history tours.

47 Plymouth Citadel Gate

The Citadel was built on the orders of Charles II to update Plymouth's defences during the Second Anglo-Dutch War, 1666. Defending Sutton Harbour in combination with artillery on Mount Batten, the Citadel's guns also faced inland. This protected it from rearward attack, but also spoke to Puritan Plymouth, which had held out through a prolonged siege for Parliament during the Civil War (1642-46). The Citadel's main gateway is decorated with Charles II's Coat of Arms.

48 Smeaton's Tower and the Hoe

Built in 1756-59, Smeaton's Tower originally stood as a lighthouse on the Eddystone Reef, 22km south of Plymouth. When the rock it stood on was eroded, Smeaton's Tower was moved block by dovetailed block to the Hoe and re-erected between 1882-84.

49 The Barbican

The Barbican is the heart of historic Plymouth. It has the largest concentration of cobbled streets in England. The Elizabethan House (National Trust, admission charge) is among an ensemble of fine timber-fronted 16th and 17th century merchants' houses in New Street. Southside Street and the 15th century Plymouth Gin Distillery should not be missed. Plymouth Mayflower (Tourist Information Centre) gives an excellent introduction to Plymouth's history with tableaux and artefacts.

50 Sutton Harbour

Sutton Harbour is Plymouth's original port. Still a busy fishing harbour and marina, with England's second largest fish market, it is also home to the National Marine Aquarium. Many former warehouses have been converted to pubs and restaurants and the old fish market to shops. Ferries to Mount Batten, Cawsand and the Royal William Yard, as well as sightseeing and fishing trips, leave from Mayflower Steps, where plaques recall many great voyages that began here.

51 Burgh Island

At low tide, visitors walk to Burgh Island across the sands from Bigbury-on-Sea, but use the sea tractor at high tide. Footpaths link the Pilchard Inn (1336), the Art Deco hotel – used as a film set for two adaptations of Agatha Christie stories – and the former medieval chapel, later used by 'huers' to alert fishermen to shoals of pilchard.

52 Salcombe and its sea tractor

South Sands also has a sea tractor which connects the beach with the Salcombe ferry, offering excellent views of the estuary, Salcombe Castle and Salcombe's quays.

53 Start Point Lighthouse

Jagged cliffs stand as Devon's southern rampart and extend beneath the turbulent seas that eddy around exposed Start Point. Over the centuries, these rocks ripped the life from many ships, especially before the lighthouse was built in 1836. Call 01803 771802 for times of guided tours of the lighthouse and visitor centre (fee).

54 Blackdown Rings

Blackdown Rings, with substantial earthen ramparts and extensive views, is a fine example of an Iron Age hillfort. In the north-west corner stands an early Norman motte and bailey castle, one of a network of castles hastily built after the 1066 Conquest and the Western Rebellion of 1068. Open all year. Free entry and parking. SX719521, TQ7 4EA. Off B3196, 3.5km (2 miles) north of Loddiswell.

55 Totnes Castle

Totnes Castle still dominates the town from every approach, just as its Norman builders intended. The original timber tower was replaced by the crenellated shell keep we can see today, augmented by its bailey and outer curtain wall. English Heritage (entry fee).

56 Totnes buildings

Tudor Totnes became Devon's second wealthiest town after Exeter. The rich cloth merchants left a remarkable heritage of Elizabethan buildings in Fore and High Streets. Several retain their steep gabled roofs and overhanging jetties, though others are partly disguised by Georgian facades. In High Street, the Butterwalk (first recorded in 1532) is an arcaded walkway.

57 Elizabethan House Museum

One of the finest buildings in Totnes is the Museum, which dates from 1575 as a merchant's house, with a ground floor shop. It is themed to the town's history and furnished with Elizabethan and Jacobean furniture, including a magnificent four poster bed. The kitchen is complete with Tudor foods and kitchen equipment. Donations requested.

58 Dartington Hall and Gardens

Dartington Hall, one of England's best late medieval buildings, is set in a beautiful mature garden with specimen trees and a great variety of flowers and shrubs, giving colour and interest through the year. Wheelchair accessible. No dogs. Donations requested.

59 Slapton Sands

Slapton Sands is a 4km (2½ mile) long shingle bar stretching from Torcross to beyond Strete Gate. Behind it is Slapton Ley, the West Country's largest freshwater lake, noted for birdwatching. Slapton Sands was a key part of the Start Bay D-Day training area, 1943-44. At Torcross, a Sherman tank stands memorial to 946 men killed in a surprise German E boat attack in 1944. It was recovered from Start Bay in 1984.

60 Dartmouth Castle

Only a tower and a portion of curtain wall remain of Dartmouth's original 1388 castle. Most of the structure dates from 1481-94, when it was redeveloped as England's first artillery fortification, designed to stop any enemy ships threatening Dartmouth. Kingswear Castle on the opposite shore completed artillery coverage, supported by a chain boom. English Heritage (admission charge).

61 Dartmouth Butterwalk

Dartmouth's Butterwalk is the finest in Devon. As at the Butterwalks in Totnes and Plympton St Maurice, a series of granite piers support the upper floors of buildings projecting over the street, providing a covered market. Dartmouth's Butterwalk consists of four splendid 17th century timber framed houses. The upper floors are profusely carved; the interiors have wonderful plasterwork, best seen in the Sloping Deck Restaurant and Dartmouth Museum.

62 Dartmouth Regatta

Held at the end of August, the Dartmouth Regatta is a packed three-day programme of sailing, rowing, sports, live music, dancing, street food and fireworks. Highlights include the Royal Regatta Ball, Illuminated Boat Procession, RNLI and Newfoundland Dog Displays and the Steamboat Rally. Dartmouth's first regatta was held in 1822. It became the Royal Regatta in 1856 when Queen Victoria and Prince Albert attended.

63 Kingswear Ferry to Ferry Walk

A fascinating and very scenic walk links Dartmouth's two ferries. Take the Lower Ferry from Dartmouth Quay to Kingswear, then the footpath which runs parallel to the Dartmouth Steam Railway upriver to the Higher Ferry, before following the riverfront pavement back to the start. Enjoy superb views of Dartmouth, Kingswear and the beautiful Dart Valley from both ferries.

64 Dittisham

The river Dart is the life and soul of Dittisham, which grew on water-borne trade and now thrives on yachting. This most attractive village has two fine inns, a medieval church and a medley of stone and slate cottages. The best way to visit is by ferry from Dartmouth, or the short crossing from Greenway Quay, close by Agatha Christie's summer home with its lovely gardens (National Trust). Extend your visit with a boat cruise upriver.

65 Berry Head fort

The headland gives tremendous views over Torbay and southwards towards Start Bay. It is a National Nature Reserve. Berry Head's Napoleonic forts defended both Torbay and the landward side of the promontory. The former guardhouse is now a café and visitor centre. Berry Head lighthouse is the highest in Britain.

66 Brixham Harbour

Busy with fishing boats and pleasure craft, Brixham Harbour always has movement and interest. As well as trawlers, crabbers and yachts, there is the *Golden Hind* – a reproduction of Sir Francis Drake's ship in which he circumnavigated the world. A wide variety of boat trips are offered from Brixham harbour.

67 Paignton Sands and Pier

Paignton is the quintessential British popular seaside resort. Ideal for children, it has a wide range of facilities, plus a long sandy beach washed by gentle waves. Enjoy whelks and ice cream on the promenade, or wrestle with a one armed bandit on the pier (free admission).

68 Cockington

Cockington, with its traditional cob and thatch cottages, has been carefully preserved as a model picturesque Devon village. Visitors can explore freely, including Cockington Court and its extensive grounds. Village buildings include the thatched forge, 17th century almshouses and the thatched Drum Inn, designed in 1936 by Sir Edwin Lutyens.

69 Torre Abbey Sands

This beach is popular with families and offers a good range of facilities. Behind the beach lie Abbey Park and Meadows, a delightful place to wander and picnic. Torre Abbey is the best preserved monastery in Devon and dates from 1196. The medieval and Georgian rooms (admission fee) house a large art collection and host regular exhibitions by contemporary artists.

70 Torquay harbour

Torquay's bustling harbour is the focal point of the town. It is sheltered by two piers and lined with a variety of shops, restaurants, bars and cafés, ideal for a leisurely promenade, or a visit to Living Coasts zoo and aquarium.

71 Hesketh Crescent

Hesketh Crescent is part of Torquay's notable heritage of Georgian and Victorian buildings. It overlooks Meadfoot beach and was built in 1846-48 for Sir Lawrence Palk, who was largely responsible for developing the Lincombe and Warberry areas of Torquay, with their handsome villas and carriage drives. Palk named the Crescent after his bride, Maria Hesketh. It is now divided into apartments, a hotel and health club.

72 Babbacombe cliff railway

The cliff railway (1926) gives a wonderful view of the Devon coast as it descends to Oddicombe beach. At 76.2m (250ft), the vertical drop is half that of the Lynton and Lynmouth railway (page 7), giving it a much gentler 35% gradient.

73 Dawlish Warren

With a long, sandy, lifeguarded beach washed by gentle currents of clear water, Dawlish Warren is ideal for families. It has a full range of facilities, plus amusement arcades and a fun fair. By contrast, the dunes are a nature reserve, with board walks, a visitor centre and bird watching hides.

74 Starcross Pumping Station

This is the best surviving feature of I K Brunel's ingenious, but financially disastrous atmospheric railway of 1847-48. Brunel sought to replace steam locomotives with static pumping stations. These created a vacuum in a continuous pipe between the rails. A hinged piston connected pipe to train and atmospheric pressure sucked it forward. A great idea but… salt air destroyed the leather flap valves and the system burned too much coal.

75 Mainline railway on coast

The exceptionally beautiful railway between Exeter and Newton Abbot follows the Exe estuary, then the coast and the Teign estuary. The coastal section includes five cliff tunnels and a four mile long sea wall. It needs frequent repairs and is sometimes closed during storms.

76 Lawrence Tower (Haldon Belvedere)

This triangular tower, at once a memorial, a luxury residence and a folly, is a prominent landmark on the crest of the Haldon Hills. Sir Robert Palk, who made his fortune in India, built the tower in 1788.

25

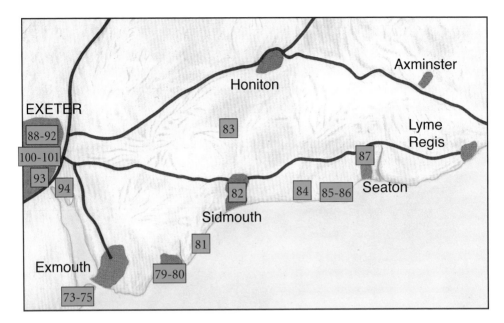

Exeter · Honiton · Axminster · Lyme Regis · Seaton · Sidmouth · Exmouth

88-92 · 100-101 · 93 · 94 · 83 · 87 · 82 · 84 · 85-86 · 81 · 79-80 · 73-75

East

77 Crediton church

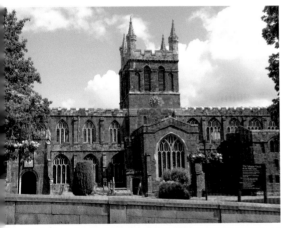

Holy Cross reflects Crediton's history as the birthplace of St Boniface. Crediton's church served as a cathedral until 1050, when the bishop's see was moved to Exeter. However, the church we see today is mainly 15th century. Look to the ceiling for carved Green Men.

78 St Peter's Church, Tiverton

St Peter's is built of an attractive mix of red sandstone and limestone, testifying to the wealth brought to Tiverton by the wool trade. Cloth merchant John Greenway financed the Greenway chapel of 1517. A series of carvings on the exterior show the ships that carried Greenway's merchandise. The interior of the chapel is also richly decorated. Another notable feature is the huge brass candelabra.

79 Budleigh Salterton beach

Large pebbles ('Budleigh Buns') give this long, steeply shelving beach its character. The Otter Estuary Nature Reserve is at the eastern end – mudflats and salt marsh noted for wildfowl and waders. Budleigh Salterton, with its mixture of Victorian villas and cottages ornés, lies behind the beach.

80 Fairlynch Museum, Budleigh

Open during the season as a local history and geology museum, Fairlynch is a classic example of a cottage orné, built in 1811 when such fancy 'cottages' were fashionable. Donations requested.

81 Ladram Bay

Ladram Bay, where the sea stacks are home to many nesting gulls, is part way between Budleigh and Sidmouth. It is one of the best places to see the New Red Sandstones so characteristic of large parts of East and South Devon. Ladram Bay has a predominantly pebbly beach with sand and rock pools at low tide, good facilities in the adjacent holiday park and easy access.

82 Sidmouth

Sidmouth's handsome sea front, flanked by huge cliffs of red sandstone, has a classic promenade, with direct access to the pebble beach. Low tide exposes sand. The town is characterised by sedate 19th century architecture, especially cottages ornés. For a week in August, Sidmouth hosts one of Britain's most noted and longest established folk festivals.

83 St Mary's, Ottery St Mary

St Mary's has twin towers and is predominantly 14th century. Its medieval clock has the Earth at the centre of the Universe and is older than the Cathedral's similar clock.

84 Branscombe

Branscombe has a thatched forge where visitors can watch smiths produce a remarkable variety of ironwork. The village also houses Devon's last traditional bakery, where the baking equipment is preserved and teas are served indoors and in the pretty garden. Both are cared for by the National Trust as is the watermill, fully restored to working order with an overshot wheel driven by water from a leat.

85 Beer Head

England's most westerly chalk cliff is an outstanding viewpoint. This white headland contrasts starkly with the older New Red Sandstones to the west and consists of calcium carbonate from the bodies of microscopic plankton, deposited during the Cretaceous period when much of Devon was submerged. Beer Stone is a locally developed hard chalk, best seen at Beer Quarry Caves and in Exeter Cathedral.

86 The Undercliffs

Hooken Undercliff is an outstanding geological feature, accessible from the Coast Path. It was formed by a massive landslip in 1790, when four hectares (9.6 acres) of land moved 60m downhill and 200m seawards after heavy rain caused the top layers of chalk and greensand to slide over the clay beneath.

87 Seaton Tramway

This electric tramway links Seaton with Colyford and Colyton along the scenic Axe valley. The tramway was opened in 1971, using the lower section of an old Southern Railway branch line from Seaton Junction that operated from 1868 to 1963. It features a variety of trams, the oldest dating from 1904.

Exeter

88 Exeter City Walls

Nearly three quarters of Exeter's city walls, which date from Roman times, still stand. Long sections founded on durable Roman masonry may be seen from several places. The walls, repaired and upgraded many times, have served the city well through many attacks and sieges, right up to the Civil War of 1642-46.

89 Guildhall

Among High Street's many historic buildings, the Guildhall is outstanding. Its massive pillared porch and carved Doric door are late Elizabethan. The huge and impressive hall with its high collar braced timber roof (1470) is hung with portraits.

90 The House That Moved

After a sustained campaign, this 15th century timber-framed merchant's house was in 1961 jacked up and moved on rollers from its original home in nearby Frog Street to prevent its destruction during road widening.

91 Exeter Cathedral

Its two massive Norman towers dominate the city's skyline but the main body of the Cathedral is 14th century. Bishop Grandisson declared it 'marvellous in beauty'. Its crowning glories are the great image screen on the west front and the magnificent ribbed vaulting of the roof.

92 Cathedral Close

Exeter's Cathedral Close has a pleasing medley of historic buildings in stone, half timbering and brick. Despite the date '1596', Number 1's façade is Victorian, but the house retains genuine 16th century features inside. Number 5's front dates from 1700, Number 6's from 1770. Numbers 7, 8 and 9a were originally medieval courtyard houses. At the time of writing, the 18th century Royal Clarence Hotel was being rebuilt after fire damage.

93 Exeter Quays

Exeter was a port even before it became the Roman regional capital; its historic quays are a delight to explore on foot.

94 Topsham

Topsham, Exeter's outport since Roman times, retains a wealth of historic buildings, mainly from 1660-1730, the period of its greatest prosperity. The oldest are on High Street and Fore Street, where 17th to 19th century façades often hide much older cores and foundations. The Strand has a remarkable collection of 17th century merchants' houses in the Dutch style.

Rainy days

95 Buckfast Abbey

The abbey was rebuilt by a small dedicated team of monks during the late 19th and early 20th centuries on the foundations of the ruined medieval abbey. It is built of local grey limestone, with golden Ham Hill stone on the exterior and Bath stone on the interior. Although most of its decorations are traditional, Buckfast Abbey is famed for its modern tall stained glass window. The site includes car parking, shops and a restaurant.

96 Princetown Visitor Centre

This is open year round with free admission. Visitors can watch films about Dartmoor, listen to oral history and enjoy a rolling programme featuring local photography and painting. Interpretive displays aided by touch screen computers bring Dartmoor's landscape, wildlife, heritage, archaeology and history vividly to life. There is a children's play area and helpful staff provide advice and information, plus a range of Dartmoor maps and books.

97 House of Marbles

The House of Marbles in Bovey Tracey is both a toy shop and a marble museum, with huge and fascinating marble runs. It is also a glass-blowing workshop, with regular displays of that art. The House of Marbles occupies the old Bovey Pottery site; it has a good museum showing the pottery's history, as well as three rare, late 19th century muffle kilns.

98 Museum of Barnstaple and North Devon

The museum tells the story of local people and landscapes. Refurbished and extended in 2019, it has a new social history gallery and a new coast explorers' gallery. Exhibits include a salmon boat, Barnstaple's 1914 horse-drawn fire engine and a 30 ft long model railway.

99 Burton Museum and Gallery, Bideford

The Burton's large, well-lit galleries feature a rolling programme of exhibitions and art workshops, with an adjacent craft gallery. Its museum sections show local life and industry. Notable exhibits include Neolithic axe heads, a large model of Bideford's medieval Long Bridge, model sailing ships and Bideford's 1573 Charter. North Devon's long established pottery industry is celebrated with a wide variety of fascinating decorated ceramics from the 17th century to the present, including many by renowned Devon potters.

100 Exeter Custom House Visitor Centre

This is Britain's oldest extant customs house, built in 1681 when Exeter's cloth trade was booming. It forms the centre of the quayside. Inside there is a sweeping staircase and beautiful plasterwork ceilings. The history and development of Exeter's Quayside is brought to life with lively displays, and an audio-visual presentation of Exeter's history.

101 Royal Albert Memorial Museum, Exeter

The Museum, built in 1865, is a handsome, solid, stone building, which gives a first class introduction to Exeter's history. Its Roman section and the preserved details from Exeter's medieval buildings are especially good. The museum's many other displays include extensive ethnographic and natural history exhibits from around the world, geology, fine art, coins and decorative art, as well as a series of special exhibitions.